A Great Idea
ENGINEERING

Burj Khalifa
The Tallest Tower in the World

By Stuart A. Kallen

NORWOODHOUSE PRESS

COVER: The Burj Khalifa rises above the city of Dubai, United Arab Emirates.

Norwood House Press
P.O. Box 316598
Chicago, Illinois 60631

For information regarding Norwood House Press, please visit our website at: www.norwoodhousepress.com or call 866-565-2900.

PHOTO CREDITS: Cover: © EmmePi Travel/Alamy; © Adrian Wilson/Beateworks/Corbis, 35; © AP Images/Express Newspapers, 42; © AP Images/Kamran Jebreeli, 41; © AP Images/Paul Beaty, 9; BASF Press Photo, 20; Bow Editorial Services, 7, 13, 16, 26; © Charles Crowell/Bloomberg via Getty Images, 36; © David Copeman/Alamy, 6; © EmmePiTravel/Alamy, 12; © Frame Focus Capture Photography/Alamy, 24, 29; © Joel Saget/AFP/Getty Images, 28; © Kam1/arabianEye/Corbis, 15; © Nasser Younes/AFP/Getty Images, 19; © Look Die Bildagentur der Fotografen GmbH/Alamy, 30, 34 © Rabih Moghrabi/AFP Getty Images, 17; © Robert Harding World Imagery/Alamy, 32 © Sean Gallup/Getty Images, 5; © Yasser Al-Zayyat/AFP/Getty Images, 38

LIBRARY OF CONGRESS CATALOGING-IN-PUBLICATION DATA

Kallen, Stuart A., 1955-
  Burj Khalifa : the tallest tower in the world / by Stuart A. Kallen.
    pages cm. -- (A great idea)
  Includes bibliographical references and index.
  Summary: "Describes how the Burj Khalifa became the tallest tower in the world and the work that went into building it. Includes glossary, websites, and bibliography for further reading"—Provided by publisher.
   ISBN 978-1-59953-598-2 (library edition : alk. paper) -
   ISBN 978-1-60357-591-1 (ebook)
1. Burj Khalifa (Dubai, United Arab Emirates)--Juvenile literature. 2. Skyscrapers--United Arab Emirates--Dubai--Juvenile literature. 3. Dubai (United Arab Emirates)--Buildings, structures, etc.--Juvenile literature. I. Title.
   NA6234.U52D8334 2013
   720'.483095357--dc23

                                                              2013010659

Manufactured in the United States of America in Stevens Point, Wisconsin.
254R—042014

Contents

Note: Words that are **bolded** in the text are defined in the glossary.

Chapter 1

The World's Tallest Tower

Sheikh Mohammed bin Rashid al Maktoum is the monarch of the oil-rich emirate of Dubai. And when Sheikh Mohammed dreams, he dreams big. The sheikh was worth about $18 billion in the early 2000s. With his money and power, Sheikh Mohammed imagined constructing the tallest building in the world.

Sheikh Mohammed was moved by ancient history. The Great Pyramid of Giza in Egypt held the title of world's tallest structure for nearly 4,200 years. Built around 2550 BC, the Great Pyramid reaches 456 feet (139m) in height. In 1647 Strasbourg Cathedral became the first building taller than the Great Pyramid. The spires of this church in Strasbourg, France, reach 466 feet (142m).

In the 20th century the height of buildings began to grow by leaps and bounds. Skyscrapers were constructed around the world. By the 1970s the tallest buildings were more than 1,400 feet (427m) tall. Most were located in the United States. In the early 2000s several record-setting skyscrapers were built in Taiwan and China.

The ruler of Dubai, Sheikh Mohammad bin Rashid al Maktoum, was inspired by the Egyptian pyramids to build the world's tallest building.

A steady flow of oil export profits has allowed Dubai to become a banking and business center and a tourist destination.

Something Sensational

Sheikh Mohammed wanted to return the world's tallest building title to the Middle East. As tourism official Jacqui Josephson states, the sheikh "wanted to put Dubai on the map with something really sensational." In early 2000 Sheikh Mohammed began planning the construction of the Burj Dubai. The building would tower over other skyscrapers. It would have a height of 2,717 feet (828m) including its spire and have 163 floors, or stories. (Burj means "tower" in Arabic, and the building would be renamed Burj Khalifa in 2010.)

World's Tallest Buildings

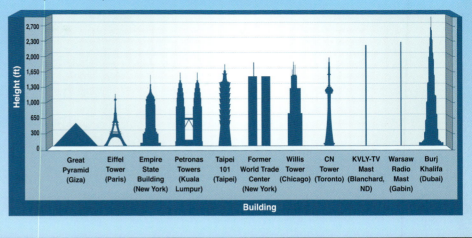

World's Tallest Buildings Compared

The Burj Khalifa compared with other well-known tall structures.

Height (ft): 2,700 / 2,300 / 2,000 / 1,650 / 1,300 / 1,000 / 650 / 300 / 0

Buildings: Great Pyramid (Giza) · Eiffel Tower (Paris) · Empire State Building (New York) · Petronas Towers (Kuala Lumpur) · Taipei 101 (Taipei) · Former World Trade Center (New York) · Willis Tower (Chicago) · CN Tower (Toronto) · KVLY-TV Mast (Blanchard, ND) · Warsaw Radio Mast (Gabin) · Burj Khalifa (Dubai)

Building

Standing at 1,250 feet (381m), the Empire State Building in New York City was the world's tallest building for more than 40 years after its completion in 1931. In 1973 the 108-story, 1,450-foot (442m) Sears Tower in Chicago entered the record books as the tallest building. Since that time, progress has been slow. Kuala Lumpur's Petronas Towers, completed in 1998, are only 33 feet (10m) taller than the Sears Tower (which was renamed the Willis Tower in 2009). The 1,670-foot (509m) Taipei 101, built in Taiwan in 2004, is 187 feet (57m) taller than Petronas Towers. The Burj Khalifa took a large leap over these former record holders. It is 1,047 feet (319m) taller than Taipei 101, reaching 2,717 feet (828m) with 163 stories. The Burj Khalifa is also more than twice as tall as the Empire State Building. When a building's height is officially calculated, the recorded height does not include spires or radio towers.

Sheikh Mohammed had more than history on his mind when he proposed the Burj Khalifa. Since the early 1960s a steady flow of crude oil has fueled the economy of Dubai. Over the years, the oil money paid for schools, hospitals, houses, and highways. However, Sheikh Mohammed wanted to make Dubai a world-class city known for more than oil production. Since the 1990s the sheikh has spent billions to remake Dubai. Today it is a tourist destination and a banking and business center.

Standing Tall in the Wind

Sheikh Mohammed turned to Skidmore, Owings, & Merrill (SOM) to design the Burj Khalifa. The Chicago-based engineering and architectural firm has designed some of the world's tallest buildings. SOM's skyscrapers include Zifeng Tower in Nanjing, China, and the Willis Tower in Chicago. However, these buildings were only about half as tall as the Burj Khalifa.

Architect Adrian Smith and **structural engineer** William F. Baker headed the SOM design team. The building had to be beautiful, but there were practical problems as well. Creative new designs were needed to build a tower half a mile tall (805m). Planners would

Architect Adrian Smith helped head up the design team for the Burj Khalifa project.

have to deal with major physical and environmental factors.

Dubai is very flat, and there is little threat from earthquakes. However, the environment is hot, humid, and extremely windy. To support the building's dizzying height in the wind, Baker invented a unique structural system called a buttressed core. A buttress is an architectural feature that supports or reinforces a wall. The buttressed core consists of a six-sided central concrete core, or hub. The building has three segments, or wings, that extend out from the buttressed core. The segments form a stable, tripod-like Y shape. The three wings of the Y shape provide wind resistance. As Baker explains, "When the wind is coming … two wings catch the wind, this third wing is the buttress. It's bracing the other parts of the building in a very natural way."

The Y shape provides strength. But a rigid building could be damaged by high winds. Like most skyscrapers, the Burj Khalifa was designed to sway slightly. In high winds the building can move as much as 6 feet (1.8m) from side to side. To monitor the movement, a global positioning system (GPS) was installed to measure the building's movement.

Sky Source Cooling

Dubai is sunny almost every day of the year and extremely humid. Keeping the giant tower cool and dry was a major challenge. Windows were designed to keep the scorching sun out of the building. They reflect the sun's rays rather than letting solar heat into the building. The 24,000 glass panels for the tower's windows equal nearly 1.3 million square feet (120,774 sq. m) of glass.

Air-conditioning the building required more inventive planning. Baker noted that air is colder at higher altitudes. This is why there is snow on top of mountains in the summer. At the building site the air at 2,700 feet (823m) was around 15°F (8°C) cooler than at ground level. To take advantage of this difference, the tower's air-conditioning system was designed to capture cool air near the top of the building. This would be pumped to warmer floors below. Baker named this new type of sys-

Ski Dubai

One of the most unusual attractions in Dubai is called Ski Dubai. It is an indoor ski resort. Ski Dubai has a 280-foot-high mountain (85m) covered in artificial snow. Skiers ride to the top on a tow lift. Although summer temperatures in Dubai can reach 119°F (48.5°C), visitors can enjoy winter skiing on five runs. There is also a sled and toboggan run and an ice body slide. Opened in 2005, the 5-acre (2.23ha) indoor winter wonderland is also home to numerous penguins, which mingle with the visitors.

tem "sky source cooling." This was combined with a traditional air-conditioning system that is used in skyscrapers.

Making the Burj Khalifa efficient and affordable to build was a world-class

Did You Know?

Dubai produces around 60,000 barrels of oil a day. That's enough to fill four Olympic-sized swimming pools.

challenge. Architects and engineers were required to create new systems that would work together and function at record heights without fail. Designing the building was only the first complex task. Construction at giddy heights would require more ingenuity. With groundbreaking scheduled for January 2004, the greatest challenges lay ahead.

Architects designed the Burj Khalifa with a six-sided concrete core in order to provide wind resistance.

Wind Tunnel Tests

When the wind blows around a skyscraper, it creates changes in air pressure. This can cause the building to buckle or crack. The Burj Khalifa needed to be tested for wind resistance. To do so, a team of engineers created a 1:500 scale model of the building. This means every 1 foot (30cm) on the model was equal to 500 feet (152m) of the structure.

The detailed replica of the Burj Khalifa was placed in a wind tunnel. This is an enclosed tubular passage with a powerful fan system.

The wind tunnel was able to mimic changes in wind speed, powerful storms, and other wind events. The effects of the wind were measured by 1,140 small holes, called pressure tabs, placed on the model. After tests, the Burj Khalifa underwent dramatic changes. The entire building design was rotated 120 degrees to reduce wind pressure on the structure. Without the wind tunnel testing, the building might have ultimately been damaged and rendered unusable.

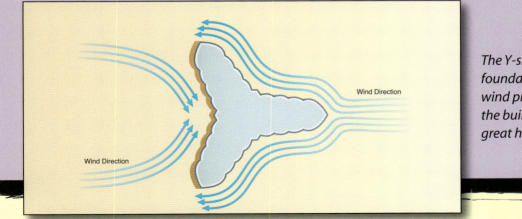

Wind Direction

Wind Direction

The Y-shaped foundation reduces wind pressure, allowing the building to soar to great heights.

Chapter 2

Construction in the Sky

Erecting the Burj Khalifa was one of the toughest building projects ever undertaken. Construction spanned six years from the digging of the foundations to the placement of the spire more than 2,000 feet (610m) above the ground. Amazing quantities of iron, glass, and concrete were manufactured. The materials were moved, shaped, and assembled by a legion of more than 12,000 skilled workers. Like a giant jigsaw puzzle with millions of pieces, the tallest building in the world rose from the desert floor.

Did You Know?

The highest temperature ever recorded in Dubai was 119 °F (48.5°C) on July 27, 2012.

The tower shattered world records as it soared into the sky.

Digging Down to Go Up

The first step in building the Burj Khalifa involved digging deep into the ground. A colossal tower needs a firm foundation. The foundation keeps the building from tilting or sinking under its massive weight. In January 2004 workers began the work. They bored 192 holes or shafts into the Arabian Desert. Each shaft was 5 feet (1.5m) wide and 164 feet (50m) deep. The shafts were filled with thick concrete columns called piles. Each pile was capable of supporting

The foundation for the tower was started in January 2004 and would take six years to complete.

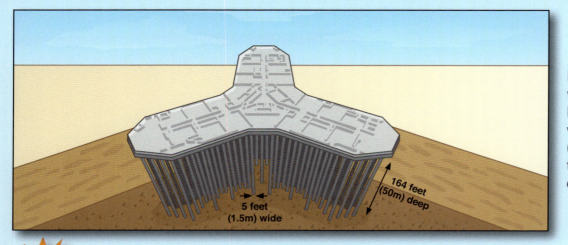

For the foundation, workers bored 192 holes each 5 feet (1.5m) wide and 164 feet (50m) deep, then filled them with concrete columns called piles.

164 feet (50m) deep

5 feet (1.5m) wide

Sagging Floors

In order to add as little weight as possible to the Burj Khalifa, the floor slabs of the building were kept as thin and light as possible. This led to problems in July 2007 when some of the floors started sagging. To fix this problem, engineers were forced to strengthen the floors with strips of a super-strong plastic material called carbon fiber. Work was completed in 2009, and the floors never sagged again.

around 3,300 tons (2,994t). Next, a huge concrete foundation called the raft was poured. The bottom floor of the building was 12 feet (3.7m) thick and shaped like a giant Y. In all, the concrete used in the foundation was equal to 1.6 million cubic feet (148,644 cu. m). This was enough concrete to fill more than 18 Olympic-sized swimming pools.

Cranes

The three tower cranes used to build the superstructure of the Burj Khalifa worked 24 hours a day. The cranes were positioned at the top of the tower as it rose from the desert floor. They were used to lift steel beams, jump frames, welding equipment, exterior cladding, and fuel for the diesel-powered cranes themselves. The cranes required 10 highly skilled operators and a team of around 25 technicians to ensure safe operation.

Installation of the cranes was relatively simple. Sections of the cranes were moved up the tower with the completion of new levels. However, getting the huge cranes back down after construction was finished was a complex task. A small recovery crane was lifted up to the 159th floor. The large cranes were dismantled and lowered to the ground by the small crane piece by piece. When this task was completed, the recovery crane was dismantled and removed by workers.

Three tower cranes were positioned at the top of the tower and rose with the building from the desert floor.

Jump Forming the Superstructure

The foundation used only about one-eighth of the concrete needed to construct the entire tower. The rest was used to form the outer sides, or superstructure, of the tower.

Work began on the walls of the superstructure in March 2005. Builders used a process known as jump forming. This method was developed for building high-rises in the 1990s. Jump forming allows quick construction of concrete walls.

The process of jump forming involves a cage, or jump form. The jump form is built from steel girders and holds panels that make up the form. The form is generally one story. It is shaped like

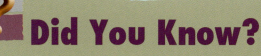

Did You Know?

Floors 44 through 108 in the Burj Khalifa are private ultra-luxury residences while office suites fill most of the remaining floors.

the building's outer walls. Concrete is poured into the form and allowed to harden for 12 hours. After one story is finished, the form is jumped (lifted) by cranes. The process is repeated on top of each finished wall. In this manner, the outer walls of the Burj Khalifa were

A photo from January 2006 shows the superstructure rising with the use of jump forming.

constructed like a wedding cake, layer upon layer.

Long, round iron bars called rebar are positioned inside each layer of concrete. Rebar adds strength to the concrete walls. The process required the use of 43,000 tons (39,000t) of rebar. Laid end to end, the rebar used on the Burj Khalifa would extend a quarter of the way around the world.

Pumping Concrete

Jump forming can be a rapid process. But builders ran into special problems when pouring concrete on the world's tallest building. Concrete is made from cement, water, and **aggregate**.

In order to pump concrete up to great heights, the BASF corporation developed a special concrete mixture that contained plastic.

Aggregate is made of coarse particles of sand, gravel, or crushed stone. These ingredients were mixed into thick liquid concrete on the ground. The concrete was then pumped up to where the jump forms were positioned.

As the Burj Khalifa grew in height, the concrete needed to be pumped higher. This process took longer and became more difficult with each rising story. No one had ever pumped concrete above 1,400 feet (427m) before. Dubai's hot and humid temperatures made the concrete thicken faster. This added another degree of difficulty.

A new type of concrete had to be invented to pump it to such record heights. The German chemical company BASF developed a special concrete mixture that contained plastic. Named Glenium Sky 504, the concrete could remain liquid for three hours. It hardened quickly once it was poured into the jump forms. To make things easier, the concrete was pumped and poured at night when temperatures were cooler. But engineers were still forced to add ice to the concrete to keep it cool.

The material was moved by massive concrete pumps run by 630 horsepower engines. These motors are as powerful as those in the fastest racecars. The machines delivered 25 tons (22.7t) of concrete at a time through pipes that reached the building's upper levels. The concrete took more than 40 minutes to reach the top floors of the tower. During the peak construction, a new floor was completed every three days.

Setting Records

By June 2006 the Burj Khalifa had grown to 50 stories. In May 2007 it had more than doubled to 107 stories. In July 2007 the tower officially became the world's tallest building when it reached 141 stories. In April 2008 the Burj Khalifa broke another record. It was taller than the 2,063-foot (629m) television transmitting antenna in Blanchard, North Dakota. This made Burj Khalifa the tallest building and the tallest human-made structure in the world.

As the top floors of the Burj Khalifa were being built, workers on lower floors began installing the outer layer of materials on the concrete walls. This protective layer, called **exterior cladding**, consisted of glass windows, which is called **glazing**. It also included stainless steel window frames called spandrel panels. The material used in the cladding was designed to resist the desert heat and sun. This improved energy efficiency in the tower and reduced the amount of air-conditioning required.

Over 300 cladding specialists, engineers, and technicians were brought in from China. The team hand cut and installed more than 24,000 glass panels and aluminum frames onto the face of the building. The total weight of the aluminum was equivalent to five Airbus A380 airplanes. These double-deck, double-wide airliners are the largest passenger jets in the world. Each cladding panel was about 21 feet by 3.8 feet (6.4m by 1.2m) and weighed 1,653 pounds (750kg).

A New Era

The complex cladding task took from May 2007 until September 2009. At first the cladding team was able to install about 25 panels a day. As work continued they installed as many as 175 panels in a single day. When finished, the area covered by the cladding on the Burj Khalifa was equal to 17 soccer fields or 25 football fields.

On October 1, 2009, the exterior of the Burj Khalifa was completed. From its foundation to the glistening windows high above the desert floor, the Burj Khalifa was a model for skyscraper builders of the future. Construction required 22 million person-hours. The total cost of the building reached more than $1.5 billion. The tower has been called a beacon of progress. And there is little doubt that Burj Khalifa represented a new era in skyscraper engineering and construction.

The Spire

A spire is a structure such as a church steeple that tapers to a point at the top. It is usually a part of a building's design created for visual appeal. The spire in the Burj Khalifa is made from 4,000 tons (3,629t) of steel. It is telescopic. That means it was created to expand after it was put in place. Once secured, the spire was jacked up to its full height of more than 660 feet (200m) with a heavy-duty lift called a strand jack. The spire also houses communications equipment for cellular networks.

The top spire was made from 4,000 tons of steel and was created to expand upwards telescopically after it was put in place.

Chapter 3

What's Inside

With its concrete superstructure finished, the Burj Khalifa was an empty shell. Workers began construction on the interior in early 2008. The task involved making the building into a vertical city. Around 12,000 people would occupy the tower's residential apartments, hotel rooms, and corporate offices.

Mechanical Floors

Some of the most important features of the Burj Khalifa are also the least beautiful. The heart of the tower consists of the mechanical, electrical, and plumbing (MEP) equipment. This provides air-conditioning, heat, running water, sanitation, lights, and power. Electrical substations, water tanks, pumps, and air-handling units are vital parts of the MEP. They are located on seven double-story floors, called mechanical floors.

While smaller buildings house mechanical floors in the basement, they are placed throughout the structure on skyscrapers. The mechanical floors provide a number of areas for pumps and equipment to keep water flowing to and from the upper floors. In the Burj Khalifa the mechanical floors are located at 30-story intervals. Each mechanical floor services 15 floors above it and 15 below. The mechanical floors also house equipment for washing the building's thousands of windows.

Water Everywhere

The Burj Khalifa consumes 250,000 gallons (946,353L) of water every day. Water for kitchens and bathrooms flows through 62 miles (100km) of pipes within the building's walls. An additional 132 miles (213km) of piping is dedicated to fire emergency sprinklers.

The complex air-conditioning system in the Burj Khalifa uses 21 miles (34km) of pipes. These transport water through the basement, where it is chilled to 38°F (3.3°C). The tower's air-conditioning relies on an ice-production system. This uses the equivalent of 14,500 tons (13,154t) of ice every day.

The cold pipes running through the warm tower walls create droplets of wastewater called condensation. (This is similar to the droplets that form on the side of a cold soda can on a hot summer day.) The condensation amounts to 18 million gallons (68 million L) of wastewater every year. According to structural engineer William F. Baker, this is enough to

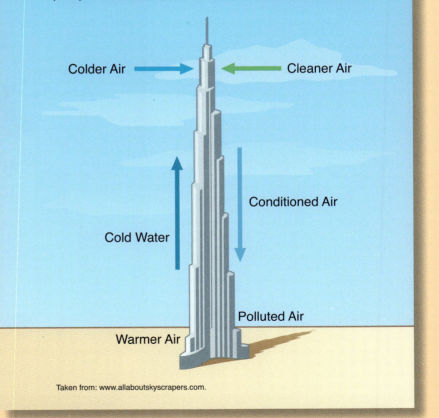

Heating, Ventilation, and Air Conditioning (HVAC) Management System

The tower's air conditioning system was designed to take advantage of colder air at higher altitudes. This system captures cool air near the top of the building and in turn pumps this cooler, cleaner air to warmer floors below.

Colder Air

Cleaner Air

Conditioned Air

Cold Water

Polluted Air

Warmer Air

Taken from: www.allaboutskyscrapers.com.

Washing 24,000 Windows

The exterior of the Burj Khalifa contains more than 24,000 windows. All need to be washed on a regular basis. Designers provided window washers with 18 permanent tracks built into the sides of the building. These hold platforms, called cradles, which are about 147 feet (45m) long. The cradles, which are stored on mechanical floors, are attached to the tracks by window washers when needed. The cradles are capable of accessing the entire facade of the tower. They move up and down on telescoping arms that extend 118 feet (36m). Using these maintenance units, washing crews can clean the entire exterior face of the Burj Khalifa in three to four months.

Equipment for washing windows is kept on maintenance floors located every 30 stories.

fill "20 Olympic-sized swimming pools of fresh water." The Burj Khalifa's air-conditioning system drains the condensation into holding tanks. The saved liquid is used to water The Park. This is a 27-acre (11ha) expanse of gardens, trees, and water features that surround the building. This system was designed specially for the Burj Khalifa. It will likely be used on skyscrapers in the future.

At the Top

Vertical transportation, or elevators, are another important aspect of the MEP. Burj Khalifa's 57 elevators are among the world's longest and fastest. Double-decker elevators whisk visitors to the

A 27-acre park with gardens, trees, and water fountains surrounds the tower.

Fifty-seven elevators travel from ground level to the observation deck, moving at speeds of 40 miles per hour. Once arriving at the observation deck, visitors can enjoy the remarkable views of downtown Dubai.

The double-decker elevators can hold up to 28 people on two levels. They are equipped with video displays and a light show. Throughout the journey to the observation deck, visitors are entertained by a multimedia presentation. The program includes the history of Dubai and the wonders of the Burj Khalifa.

Other elevators in the Burj Khalifa are dedicated for residential floors, hotel rooms, and corporate offices. People traveling to these areas cannot take a

124th-floor observation deck, called At the Top. The observation deck is 1,483 feet (452m) above the ground. The elevators move at a record-setting 40 miles per hour (64kph), or 59 feet (18m) per second and the trip to At the Top takes less than one minute.

Trapped in the Elevator

The elevator to At the Top, the observation deck in the Burj Khalifa, is one of the longest in the world. In February 2010, just a month after the grand opening of the tower, the elevator was at the center of a frightening incident. About 60 visitors were on the 124th-floor observation deck when a loud crash rang out. This was followed by the sound of breaking glass. People began to panic when dust billowed out from between the elevator doors.

The elevator, with 15 passengers inside, had broken down. The lights went out, and the elevator cab fell several stories before the emergency brakes kicked in. Emergency crews had to pry open the elevator doors. They dropped a ladder down to the cab, which was trapped between floors. No one was hurt. But passengers were shaken after spending 45 minutes trapped in the dark elevator. People who remained on the observation deck had to be taken down on a maintenance elevator. The Burj Khalifa was temporarily closed to the public until issues with the elevator's electrical system were fixed.

single elevator ride to their destinations. Instead, express elevators move people from the ground to what are called sky lobbies. The sky lobbies are on levels 43, 76, and 123. Passengers in sky lobbies can transfer to local elevators that stop at every floor above. For those who prefer to walk, the Burj Khalifa has 2,909 stairs from the ground to level 160, the topmost habitable floor.

Safety First

Perhaps the most important elevator in the Burj Khalifa is the service elevator. This elevator is used by maintenance workers to move equipment to mechanical floors. It is also available in case of emergency

The Park

The Burj Khalifa is surrounded by an open space known as The Park. This is fed with water generated by the tower's massive air-conditioning system. The Park features walking paths, outdoor dining, a lookout, a forest grove, a play area, and six fountains. The 30-acre (12ha) human-made Burj Khalifa Lake is a central feature of The Park. The Dubai Fountain in the middle of the lake displays a music, water, and light show. The fountain features 6,600 lights and 25 color projectors that illuminate jets of water shooting up a record-setting 500 feet (152m) into the air in various patterns. The waters dance while Arabic and world music plays on a state-of-the-art sound system.

The Park includes the Dubai Fountain, which displays music, water, and a light show.

to transport firefighters and firefighting equipment to floors throughout the building. The elevator can lift 12,000 pounds (5,443kg) to the upper reaches of the tower. In 2010 it was the world's longest elevator ride, rising to nearly 1,655 feet (504m).

In case of fire or terrorist attack, the service elevator is used for what is called "lifeboat evacuation." During evacuation mode, firefighters and trained staff shuttle people to specially equipped emergency rooms. These are located about every 25 floors. The emergency rooms are super-reinforced, pressurized, and air-conditioned. They are sealed from outside smoke or airborne toxins. The rooms are fireproof and have their own sources of oxygen.

Crisis Command

The emergency system includes sensors placed throughout the building. These monitor smoke, heat, building cracking, and other problems. In emergency situations, the system immediately notifies occupants. It uses an alarm and voice system that communicates in Arabic and English. Flat-panel video screens in key locations display emergency information.

The Burj Khalifa also employs a Crisis Command Team trained to respond to emergencies. According to fire protection consultant Bassel Mehio, "A team, which will be onsite 24 hours a day, seven days a week has been trained and briefed on what to do in all situations whether it's a fire [or] earthquake."

from the sprinklers does not fill up the shaft. These features ensure elevators remain functional during emergencies.

Final Touches

In the final weeks before the opening, workers fitted out the interior with features that made the Burj Khalifa a symbol of luxury and comfort. The floors in the lobby were covered with expensive stone tiles. Floors in the halls were covered with fine, handmade

A massive sprinkler system snakes throughout the entire building. This activates when a fire breaks out. Elevator shafts are encased in fireproof concrete. These are outfitted with sills so that water

One thousand luxury apartments are available for lease in the Burj Khalifa.

carpet. Walls were coated with Venetian stucco. This is a type of plaster made from marble dust that is polished to a high gloss. The final wall decorations consisted of more than 1,000 pieces of art. The artwork was made by prominent Middle Eastern and international artists.

The task of plastering, painting, and decorating the 1,000 residential apartments in the Burj Khalifa was handled by the American company Depa. The Burj Khalifa was finished inside and out by the end of 2009. Within months it would become a busy city in the sky, providing homes, jobs, and hotel rooms to tens of thousands of people every day.

Chapter 4

A Milestone and a Stepping-Stone

The official opening ceremony for the Burj Khalifa was held on January 4, 2010. The date was almost exactly six years from the date work had begun on the foundation. During the launch party, more than 10,000 fireworks

During the official opening ceremony for the Burj Khalifa, more than 10,000 fireworks were exploded around the tower.

Burj Khalifa Urban Legends

The Burj Khalifa set many world records. The tall tower also generated its share of urban myths and legends. These are stories that sound amazing but are simply not true. Some of the urban legends include:

- The Burj Khalifa is so tall that nothing within a 6-mile (10km) radius will ever be struck by lightning again.

- A construction worker, known only as Dev, set the unofficial record for the Burj Khalifa vertical marathon, running up the building's 2,909 stairs in 23 minutes and 45 seconds.

- The crane operator lived in the cab of his crane at the top of the Burj Khalifa for the duration of the construction.

- More levels can be added to the Burj Khalifa at a later date so it can retain its record-setting height.

- The Burj Khalifa can be seen from outer space.

exploded around the tower. Nearly 900 powerful strobe lights pulsed on and off. Lasers bathed the tower in dramatic shadows and light while music played. Dubai Fountain shot dancing waters high into the air. Parachute jumpers drifted down from the sky. Sheikh Mohammed had achieved his dream of constructing the world's tallest building. But not everything had gone according to plan.

A Change of Names

During the six years the tower was under construction, the building was called Burj Dubai. Even on the day of its grand opening, the building's website continued to use that name. And the area around the building, with its parks and

grand opening. This was done to honor Sheikh Khalifa bin Zayed al Nahyan. Sheikh Khalifa is the emir of the conservative, oil-rich Abu Dhabi, located next door.

It later came to light that Dubai was nearly bankrupt in November 2009. The emirate was unable to make payments on a $60 billion dollar loan. Dubai had to be rescued by a $20 billion bailout from Sheikh Khalifa. In return, the Burj Dubai was renamed the Burj Khalifa.

The economic problems facing Dubai were not unusual. When work began on the Burj Khalifa, home and commercial

shopping mall, was referred to as Downtown Burj Dubai. But the name was suddenly changed to Burj Khalifa for the

building prices were climbing higher every month. This resulted in housing prices reaching a peak in 2006. In 2007 there was a sharp decline in housing and other real estate prices in the United States, Europe, Asia, and the Middle East. This caused an economic crisis known as the Great Recession.

Tall and Empty

Between 2008 and 2009 Dubai went from being the world's best property market to one of the worst. As a result of the real estate crash, prices in Dubai fell by 50 percent. This sparked a debt crisis that was called the "Dubai shock." Thousands of apartments and office spaces in Dubai's skyscrapers were left vacant. By the time Burj Khalifa opened, the world's tallest building was only half full. According to critic Steven Zeitchik, this led some to say that "the Burj Khalifa is not only the world's tallest building but also its emptiest."

By 2012 the world economy had improved and with it, the fortunes of the Burj Khalifa did as well. About 800 of the building's 1,000 apartments were occupied. However, 20 floors of office space were vacant. Part of the problem was traced to the building's design. With its long, spindly design, floor space is limited in the Burj Khalifa. Large companies that occupy office space in an average skyscraper can put all their offices on one floor. In the Burj Khalifa, companies needed to rent several floors, which is very expensive.

Record-Setting Achievements

Whatever the real estate market, Burj Khalifa officially remained the world's tallest building and tallest freestanding structure. With 163 floors, it had the highest number of stories and the highest occupied floor. The building was also the tallest structure to include residential living space.

Several records were set during construction. In November 2007 workers set a world record for pumping concrete. While forming the superstructure of the building, concrete was poured at 1,972 feet (601m). This was followed by a new world record

BASE Jumping

BASE jumpers are people who get thrills by strapping parachutes to their backs and jumping off tall buildings, antennas, bridges, and cliffs. Little wonder the Burj Khalifa attracted several daring BASE jumpers. However, jumping from the Burj Khalifa without permission is strictly illegal. This did not stop French BASE jumper Hervé Le Gallou and his British partner, David McDonnell, from leaping off the world's tallest building. They did so in May 2008, two years before the tower was finished. To bypass Burj Khalifa security, the men dressed as European engineers who had come to work on the site. As the sun came up, McDonnell jumped off a balcony on the 158th floor. Le Gallou was caught and arrested by security. However, it was later revealed that Le Gallou had successfully made the jump in secret a week earlier. He had posted a video made with a helmet camera on the Internet to prove his accomplishment. In January 2010 authorities gave permission to BASE jumpers Nasr al Niyadi and Omar al Hegelan. They leaped from the 160th floor of the Burj Khalifa. This broke the previous world record for the highest BASE jump.

A diner can get a panoramic view of Dubai from The Atmosphere restaurant, which sits on the 122nd floor of the tower. It is the world's highest restaurant.

for the highest installation of exterior cladding. Aluminum and glass panels were installed at 1,680 feet (512m).

When the Burj Khalifa opened, At the Top was the highest outdoor observation deck in the world. The elevator to the deck was the longest of any in the world. On a clear day, visitors to At the Top can see for 50 miles (80km).

The eatery Atmosphere, located on the 122nd floor, holds the record for the world's highest restaurant. The highest nightclub is on the 144th floor of the Burj Khalifa. The world's second-highest swimming pool is on the 76th floor.

As the tallest building in the world, the Burj Khalifa has attracted Hollywood filmmakers. The building was used as a backdrop for exciting stunts shot for the 2011 movie *Mission: Impossible—Ghost Protocol*. The building has also attracted several BASE jumpers. These are extreme-sports lovers who dive off tall buildings with parachutes strapped to their backs.

Mission: Impossible

In November 2010 the Burj Khalifa was used as a backdrop for exciting scenes in the movie *Mission: Impossible—Ghost Protocol*. The character Ethan Hunt, played by actor Tom Cruise, leaps out a window on the 134th floor of the Burj Khalifa. He moves across the building and crashes through a window on the 112th floor. Cruise did his own stunts. He wore a harness with safety wires as he jumped, rappelled, climbed, and ran across the face of the Burj Khalifa more than 1,300 feet (396m) in the air. A nearby helicopter filmed the action, which took place over the course of several days. *Mission: Impossible—Ghost Protocol* was released in 2011.

Actor Tom Cruise hangs from the Burj Khalifa's cladding while filming a scene for the film Mission Impossible: Ghost Protocol.

"We Could Easily Do a Mile"

Records are made to be broken. The Burj Khalifa will not remain at the top for long. Only ten months after the tower was open, ground was broken in Kuwait for the Burj Mubarak al Kabir. When finished in 2017, the tower will be 3,284 feet (1,001m) tall. The building has a price tag of more than $7.5 billion. It will stand 567 feet (173m) taller than the Burj Khalifa.

There is little doubt that architects are already making plans to exceed the Burj Mubarak. As structural engineer William F. Baker commented about the Burj Khalifa, "We could go twice that [high] or more…. We could easily do a kilometer. We could easily do a mile. We could do at least a mile and probably quite a bit more." Whether or not people need buildings that reach a mile into the sky might be beside the point. With a new generation of record-breaking buildings, humanity will continue to push toward the stars—with jump forms, concrete pumps, and double-decker elevators leading the way.

Glossary

aggregate [AG-re-get]: An ingredient of concrete, this substance is made from sand, gravel, crushed stone, dirt, or other coarse material.

architect [AR-ka-tekt]: A person who plans and designs buildings and oversees their construction.

exterior cladding [EX-teer-e-or KLAD-ing]: The protective material on the outer face of a building, including windows and bricks.

glazing [GLA-zing]: A construction term used for the glass windows of a building and also for the act of installing the windows.

structural engineer [STRUCK-sher-al in-gin-EER]: A person who designs and analyzes the physical components of a building to safely withstand the forces of gravity, earthquakes, wind, heat, storms, and other factors.

For More Information

Books

Kaite Goldsworthy
  Burj Khalifa with Code. New York:
  Av2 by Weigl, 2012.

Michael Hurley
  *The World's Most Amazing
  Skyscrapers*. Mankato, MN: Raintree,
  2012.

Lisa McCoy
  United Arab Emirates. Broomall, PA:
  Mason Crest, 2010.

David Orme
  Skyscrapers. Winchester, UK:
  Ransom, 2012.

Alex Woolf
  Buildings: Design and Engineering.
  Mankato, MN: Heinemann, 2013.

Websites

All About Skyscrapers, Burj Khalifa
www.allaboutskyscrapers.com/property/
burj-khalifa-2

Burj Khalifa
www.burjkhalifa.ae

Dubai: 10 Things To Do
www.time.com/time/travel/cityguide/
article/0,31489,1849667,00.html

Virtual Tour of Dubai City
www.airpano.ru/files/UAE-Dubai-City-
Virtual-Tour/2-2

What's the New Tallest Building in the World?, HowStuffWorks
http://adventure.howstuffworks.com/burj-
dubai1.htm

Index

About the Author

Stuart A. Kallen is the author of more than 250 books for children and young adults. His titles have covered subjects ranging from history, art, and music to ghosts, vampires, and ESP. Kallen lives in San Diego, where he hikes, bikes, and plays music in his spare time.